THAT'S ME IN HISTORY

MEDIEVAL ENGLAND

Ann Tatlock

PURPLE TOAD
PUBLISHING

P.O. Box 631
Kennett Square, Pennsylvania 19348
www.purpletoadpublishing.com

That's Me in History

ANCIENT EGYPT
MEDIEVAL ENGLAND
MING DYNASTY CHINA
RENAISSANCE ITALY
THE SPANISH EMPIRE: THE INQUISITION

PUBLISHER'S NOTE: The data in this book has been researched in depth, and to the best of our knowledge is factual. Although every measure is taken to give an accurate account, Purple Toad Publishing makes no warranty of the accuracy of the information and is not liable for damages caused by inaccuracies.

ABOUT THE AUTHOR: Ann Tatlock is the author of ten novels. Her works have received numerous awards, including the Silver Angel Award from Excellence in Media and the Midwest Book Award. She lives in the Blue Ridge Mountains of Western North Carolina with her husband, daughter, three Chihuahuas, and a guinea pig named Lilly.

Printing 1 2 3 4 5 6 7 8 9

Publisher's Cataloging-in-Publication Data
Tatlock, Ann
   Medieval England / Ann Tatlock
      p. cm. – (That's me in history)
Includes bibliographical references and index.
ISBN: 978-1-62469-000-6 (library bound)
1. Great Britain – History – Medieval period, 1066-1485 – Juvenile literature. 2. England – Civilization – 1066-1485 – Juvenile literature.   I. Title.
  DA175.T38 2013
  942.03—dc23
                                        2012955618

eBook ISBN: 978-1-62469-011-2

Printed by Lake Book Manufacturing, Chicago, IL

CONTENTS

INTRODUCTION:
Fire!

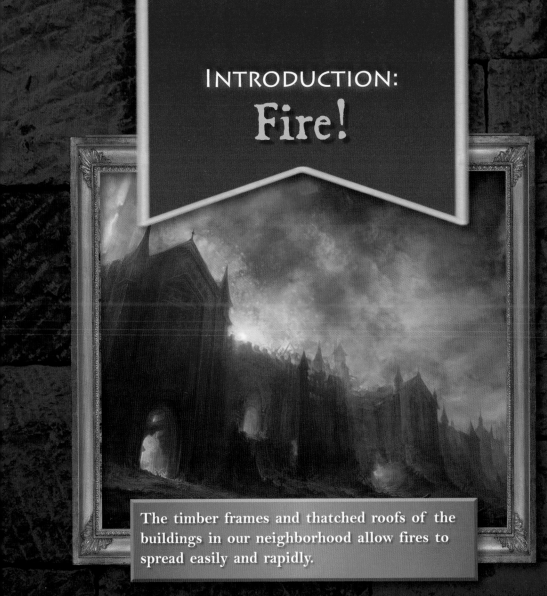

The timber frames and thatched roofs of the buildings in our neighborhood allow fires to spread easily and rapidly.

Listen, the bells!

Father, John, and I look up from our work in alarm. Father stops raking the coals in the oven. John stops kneading the dough. I stop sweeping the floor. The bells in our city ring many times a day, but right now it isn't dawn and it isn't curfew and it isn't time to pray.

Something's wrong!

People begin to rush through the street past our bakery.

"Fire!" someone yells. "Fire! Fire!"

Father unties his apron. "Come on, William," he says. "You too, John

We each grab a bucket and join the others running through the street. In a crowded city like ours, fire is one of the biggest threats and greatest dangers. One tipped-over candle or wayward spark from the fireplace can make a whole section of the city go up in flames. When a fire starts, it's everyone's duty to grab a bucket of water and help put it out.

Come on! I know it's hard to run through these narrow winding streets filled with people, horses and carts, but we must hurry. The streets are unpaved and uneven and full of garbage and . . . watch out for the pigs! Be careful not to trip over anything or fall into the rubbish people have thrown out their upper-floor windows. And try not to step into the open drain running down the center of the street. That's where people throw their dirty water.

As we turn first one way and then another, the streets are becoming narrower until they are little more than alleys. This is the poorest section of the city with the poorest houses. You can see how old they are, with their shutters hanging at odd angles and their shingles slipping from the roofs. Because these single-story houses are built from old timber, fire starts easily and spreads quickly.

As soon as we round this corner, we'll be there. Do you smell the smoke? Look, the flames! Father, John, and I join the bucket brigade, dipping water out of the tubs outside of each small house. Others are carrying water up from the river. Do you see those men with the long-handled tools with hooks on the ends? Those are fire hooks. The men are using them to pull the burning roof off the house that's on fire. They're also pulling down the houses next to the house on fire so the flames don't spread.

With everyone working together, we should have the fire out soon. I think we'll be lucky this time and only a few small houses will be lost rather than a whole street or neighborhood. As soon as we know it's safe to go home, meet me back at the bakery and I'll tell you all about what life is like in an English city in the year 1302.

CHAPTER 1
Home and Family

Hello, again! Come on in. Now that the fire's out, and everyone is going about his daily business again, I can show you around.

My name is William and, at ten years of age, I'm the eldest son in my family. My father is a baker, and we live here on Baker Street. You can probably tell that the people who live on this street are bakers from the signs out front of each shop that look like loaves of bread.

That's my father pulling the bread out of the oven with the long wooden paddle. The young man kneading the dough is Father's apprentice, John. Father is teaching him everything he needs to know to own a bakery himself one day.

I'll tell you more about what it's like to be a baker, but first follow me. I'll show you our home behind the bakery. It's a simple home, nothing like the fancy homes where the rich merchants live in another part of the city. And not at all like the manor homes and castles that nobles and barons live in! Our home is

The streets of a medieval English town are a constant bustle of activity as people from nobles to peasants go about their daily lives.

The home's main room is sparsely furnished and serves as both living space and kitchen. The homemaker hangs herbs to dry from the ceiling and cooks over an open fire in the middle of the room.

made out of mud bricks and wood, and instead of windows we have only small slits in the walls to let air in. Many buildings like castles and cathedrals have glass windows, but sometimes even wealthy families have only oiled parchment as window coverings instead of glass. We don't have parchment or glass because we can't afford them. But still, we have everything we need and we're comfortable.

Some of the poorest families in our city live in only one room, but we have three rooms—the main room and two small bedrooms. We don't have much furniture, just a few chairs, a three-legged stool, a trestle table where we eat, two wooden chests, and a cradle for the baby. In each bedroom we have mattresses stuffed with straw, and a washstand. We keep our clothes, sheets and woolen blankets in the chests.

To go to the bathroom, we use the outhouse in the back yard. At night we use chamber pots that we must empty in the morning. We share a well with several other houses, so every day we carry in water for drinking, cooking, and washing. Our city is large enough to have a public bathhouse, but still we generally take a bath only once a week. It's hard to keep ourselves and our house clean because of fleas, lice, and bedbugs. Rats are also frequent visitors to our house!

Our cooking fire is in the center of the main room and the smoke escapes through a hole in the roof. This fireplace is very important because it gives us warmth and light. It's also where Mother prepares our food. Our food is simple. We live off bread, of course, and vegetable stews made from cabbage, onions, garlic, lentils, peas, and beans. We have a small garden out back where Mother grows vegetables and herbs. Occasionally we eat eggs, cheese, and meat, though only the wealthy are able to eat meat often. We also eat fresh fruit like apples and cherries that we buy in the marketplace, but most fruit has to be dried so it lasts longer. We drink goat's or ewe's milk, and ale made from barley or mead made from honey. Honey is also the most common way of sweetening food.

Mother cooks in the cauldron that is hanging over the fire. She uses wooden spoons and pottery bowls, and she has a pestle and mortar for grinding and crushing herbs. We also have some pewter plates and brass pots, but these are used only on special occasions. Even though we have spoons, we mostly eat with our hands.

Meals are prepared in cauldrons, heavy metal pots that hang over the fire.

Now, let's tiptoe over to the cradle and peek in. That's my little brother Harvey! He's six months old. You may wonder why he's wrapped up tightly in cloth like that. Those are called swaddling clothes. See, most parents are afraid that their children's bodies will grow crooked, so they wrap them up tightly to help them grow straight and tall. When a baby is old enough to sit up by himself, he will wear regular clothes.

Babies are born at home with the help of midwives but without doctors. Many babies die at birth. Many mothers die also. Because of disease, starvation, and accidents, about half of all children die before the age of five years old.

But those who live will spend their early childhood playing. See the little girl playing on the floor with her rag doll? That's my sister Elizabeth. She's three years old. When she's older she'll help Mother with the cooking, cleaning, and sewing, just as I help Father in the bakery now. But still, as children we enjoy playing with hoops, balls, kites, spinning tops, wooden swords, and stilts. Some kids, mostly peasant children, have fun with balloons made from the bladders of slaughtered pigs. We also like to play games like checkers, chess, backgammon, lawn bowling, and blind man's bluff.

Children play with barrels, hobby horses, and hoops, which are large rolling wooden rings pushed along with sticks.

A medieval professor and his students study such subjects as mathematics, science, theology (study of religion) and the arts.

Most of us children won't get any formal education. While there are schools, not everyone is allowed to go to them. Most schools are for boys only. Many are run by the Church, and the boys who attend them are expected to become monks or priests. Some girls are sent to convents and learn to become nuns, though most girls learn housekeeping and are readied for marriage and motherhood. The boys and girls who do receive education are usually the children of nobles and wealthy merchants.

Boys who are peasants will work the land like their fathers do, and those of us whose fathers are craftsmen will also learn a trade and become craftsmen. Soon I'll become an apprentice to a craftsman so I can learn a trade. My father has already made the arrangements with a friend of his who is a carpenter. I will learn how to be a carpenter in the way John is learning how to be a baker.

Come back into our bakery and I'll tell you more about making a living in our town, in our time.

Why "The Dark Ages"?

Sometimes the Middle Ages are called "The Dark Ages." This term was first used by the scholars and writers of the Italian Renaissance. The Renaissance was a movement that arose toward the end of the Middle Ages when creative people began to take a new interest in the ancient learning of the Greeks and Romans. These people, called humanists, believed they were starting a new age, one far better than any in the previous ten centuries. In looking back over the Middle Ages, Renaissance thinkers saw that time as dark and barbaric, a time in which no real growth happened. But this isn't true.

The Middle Ages began around 476 with the fall of the Roman Empire. At one time Rome ruled much of Europe, but when its power was broken, tribes from Northern Europe started moving into old Roman lands and setting up new kingdoms. War raged for several centuries. Many villages, towns, and cities were pillaged and ransacked. So it's true that during this time, libraries and other records were destroyed and things people knew in earlier times were lost or forgotten. But by 900, things began to settle down and society began to arrange itself in new ways.

The government that formed came to be known as feudalism. The most powerful people in Western Europe were the nobles. These were the kings and the lords who controlled large areas of land. In order to protect their lands they gave smaller areas of land, called fiefs, to lesser nobles who promised to obey and protect their lords in exchange for the land. These lesser nobles, called vassals, raised knights to fight for the kingdom. The people who farmed the land to provide food for the

The Black Death claimed hundreds of thousands of lives all across fourteenth-century Europe.

kingdom were called peasants. The feudal system looked like a pyramid with the king on top, the great lords, lesser nobles, and knights in the middle, and the majority of the people, the peasants, on the bottom.

Eventually, towns and cities grew in population, trade bloomed within England and many other countries, and a new class of people arose. This new middle class included merchants, skilled craftspeople and others like doctors, lawyers, and bankers. At the same time universities were built, hospitals began to appear, and new inventions moved society forward.

Still, life in the fourteenth century when our friend William lived was filled with hardship and natural disasters. Toward the end of the thirteenth century, Europe entered a "Little Ice Age" in which the weather was very wet and cold. Crops failed and many people died over the 25-year famine that followed. Later in the fourteenth century the plague known as the Black Death spread across Europe many times killing hundreds of thousands of people. In 1337, Europe saw the beginning of the Hundred Years War between England and France. With famine, plague, and war, life was very hard indeed.

CHAPTER 2
Work and Livelihood

Here in the bakery, our workday begins early in the morning, even before the sun comes up. Our work is very important because we make the food that is the staple of everyone's diet: bread. Every man, woman, and child eats an average of 12 pounds of bread a week.[1] Not only do we make and sell our own bread, but because peasants and regular townspeople don't have ovens in their homes, they sometimes bring their dough to us for baking.

Before daybreak, Father takes our grain to the miller so it can be ground into flour to make the bread. John, our apprentice, cleans out the ovens, adds wood to the firebox and rakes the coals to adjust the heat. Father begins kneading the dough and setting it to rise. I take the buckets and run to the well to bring back water.

We make several different kinds of bread. The finest bread and biggest loaves are made from wheat flour.[2] We make what are called trenchers, which are thick slices that are used

An apprentice watches and learns while a baker slips loaves of bread dough into the oven using a long wooden paddle.

Trencher bread

instead of plates to hold food. We also make twice-baked bread, which is like crackers.

As bakers, we are only one of the many kinds of craftsmen who work in the city. If you take a little walk with me through the streets, I'd like to point out the shop signs to you. Because many people can't read, shop owners have painted signs outside their shops with pictures to let people know what they sell.[3] See the sign with the scissors? That's a cloth shop. The pestle and mortar on the next sign means that shop is a pharmacy. When we take our grain to the miller, we see that his sign has a bushel of wheat. The butcher's has a cut of meat and the blacksmith's has an anvil and hammer.

The city is buzzing as people work their different jobs. As you walk through the city streets, you'll see cobblers, candlemakers, fishmongers, spinners, weavers, stonemasons, architects, engineers, inventors, glassblowers, teachers, clerks, painters, and playwrights. Some people work in the castle, like heralds, archers, chamberlains, butlers, and servants.

A few people have a mix of jobs, like the barber. Not only does he cut hair, but he also acts as a surgeon, pulling teeth, setting broken bones, and even cutting off infected arms and legs! Then there's the

A barber-surgeon tends to the arm of a wounded man with the help of his apprentice.

minstrel. He's the man standing on the street corner, singing and playing the lute. He's something of a traveling musician, making his way from town to town. Not only does he write songs and sing, but also he tells stories and does acrobatics.

And look! See the man there ringing the hand bell? He's the town crier. He wanders through the streets calling out the news and making announcements. We all stop to listen when we hear his bell and his cry of "Oyez, oyez!" This is the way we find out what's happening in and around the city.

So many jobs! Still, people don't have much choice in the work they do. It mostly depends on their station in life; that is, the class into which they were born. Many people are born peasants and will remain peasants all their lives. They live outside the walls of the city and farm the land. The only way they can break out of their station is if they flee

A woman herding sheep on a farm outside town wears the headscarf and tunic common to the peasant class.

to another town or city and survive there for a year and a day. If they manage to avoid capture, they become freemen. Then, once they become longtime residents and help with the town's civic life, they can become citizens. But this is very rare.

While many people in the city are merchants and craftsmen, most are unskilled laborers. Some have no regular jobs but simply try to find work day by day. Others work as servants by cooking, cleaning, and helping in businesses. Still others are involved in farming and leave the city every day to work in fields, orchards, vineyards, and pastures. At night they return to the city before the guards close the gate.

However people earn a living, we all work hard. The normal workday is ten to fourteen hours long, and unless there's a holiday during the week, our only day off is Sunday.

Even the wealthy and powerful people—the nobility—have work to do. If you are born a noble, you will grow up to do the work of a noble. Or you might be a member of the clergy or some other kind of worker in the church, and all these people have their various tasks to do as well. But I will tell you more about these jobs when we talk about life in the castles and in the Church.

Most of the merchants and craftsmen, like my father, belong to guilds. The Merchant Guilds and the Craft Guilds are separate but similar. They were formed in order to control the price of goods, people's wages, the quality of the product, and the people's working conditions. Even women are allowed to join the guilds as butchers, bookbinders, shoemakers, and such. Domestic activities such as brewing, spinning, and silk making are done only by women.

Many of the wealthier guilds offer a welfare system in the city. They build schools, feed the poor, run retirement homes, watch after widows and orphans, and give money to members who are too sick to earn a living.

Craft guilds are ruled by master craftsmen, like my father, who have their own shops. The journey to become a master craftsman is done in three parts. First, Father was an apprentice like John is now and like I

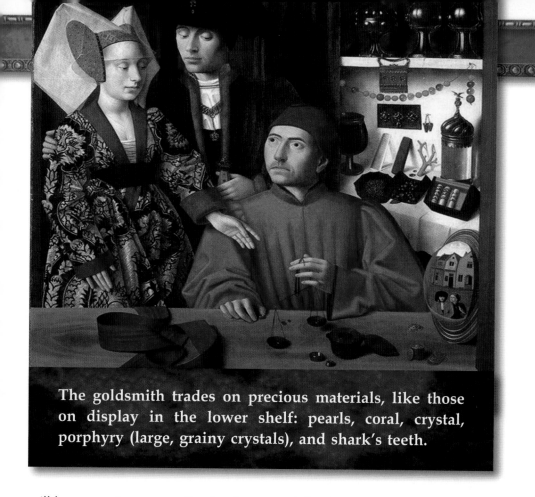

The goldsmith trades on precious materials, like those on display in the lower shelf: pearls, coral, crystal, porphyry (large, grainy crystals), and shark's teeth.

will be soon. An apprentice is given special training as well as food and a place to sleep. He works hard but is not paid. In fact, his father or someone else has to pay the master a fee for the time he spends training the apprentice.

An apprenticeship lasts about seven years. By this time the boy is a young man and he becomes what is called a journeyman. He travels from town to town and works for different masters to gain experience. After several years, he can join a guild. Eventually he will pay a fee and present a "masterpiece" to show his skill. If the guild accepts the masterpiece, the journeyman becomes a master craftsman and can open his own shop and take on apprentices of his own.

Someday, years from now, I hope to create a masterpiece that will allow me to join the Carpenter's Guild. I want to have my own shop where I can build all sorts of things that will be both useful and beautiful.

Great Inventions of the Middle Ages

Over the centuries, many important inventions made work and life a little easier for people throughout Europe. Let's take a look at eight of those inventions.

Fifth Century—The Heavy Plow. The heavy plow was mounted on wheels and drawn by several oxen. The wheels allowed the plow to be adjusted to different heights according to how shallow or deep the farmer wanted his furrows. With the wheels, the farmer didn't have to hold up the weight of the plow with his own strength, so plows could be heavier and could more easily till the weighty soils of northern Europe. This important invention led to greater food production.[4]

Ninth Century—Bells. Skilled metal-working methods allowed for the production of the first metal bells in Europe. Bells were used for such purposes as calling people to prayer, signaling curfews, and alerting people to dangers such as fires.

Twelfth Century—Windmill. Along with learning to use the power of water, inventors in the Middle Ages learned to use the power of wind. Many windmills were built in Europe from about 1100 onward, and the mills were used to grind corn into flour.

Thirteenth Century—The Mechanical Clock. Before clocks, people used "solar time." That is, they used such devices as sundials to determine how far the sun had traveled across the sky. Soon, though, mechanical clocks, known as turret clocks, were built into the bell towers of castles, abbeys, and cathedrals. These clocks used hands to point to the hour and minute. When clocks came about, people still used solar time, so it was important to say "hour of the clock" when talking about the time given on a turret clock. This saying became shortened to "o'clock," which is what we say today.[5]

Windmill

Spinning
Wheel

Gutenberg's
Press

Spinning Wheel. A spinning wheel is a machine used for spinning thread or yarn from natural fibers like cotton, wool, and hemp. It replaced hand spinning with a spindle and distaff and greatly advanced the cloth industry.[6]

Eyeglasses. The invention of eyeglasses was made possible when glassmakers learned how to make clear glass. The first glasses had convex lenses which improved vision for the farsighted. Concave lenses which helped the nearsighted, did not appear until the sixteenth century.[7]

Fourteenth Century—Water-powered Blast Furnace. The production of iron was greatly improved with the invention of the water-powered blast furnace. Furnaces had long been used in changing the raw material of iron ore into usable iron. Now, a waterwheel was used to pump a pair of huge bellows that blew air into the furnace which increased the draft and raised the temperature of the fire. This new system made much more iron with much less labor.[8]

Fifteenth Century—The Printing Press of Gutenberg. When Johannes Gutenberg, a silversmith by trade, invented the printing press, he made it possible for books to be mass produced fairly quickly and easily. For the first time in history, both the educated class and middle class had a world of knowledge at their fingertips. This changed the way people learned and paved the way for the advances in technology that followed.[9]

CHAPTER 3
The Church and Society

Listen, the bells! This time they aren't ringing because of a fire. The church bells are calling the people to pray, just as they do seven times a day. Usually, though, only the monks and nuns pray at every bell.

Still, the church is central to everyone's life, with special ceremonies to mark each important occasion. Remember my baby brother Harvey? When he was born he was taken to the church and baptized by the priest. When he's older, he will go through confirmation and become a full member of the church, just as we all do. Mother and Father were married by the priest at the door of the church, with God, their families, and friends as witnesses. When Grandfather was sick and about to die, the priest came and heard his last confession. Then he was buried in the cemetery

Simple parish churches built of stone and mortar dot the English countryside and their bells call the townsfolk to worship. St. Martin's Church, above, in Canterbury, England, was used by St. Augustine in the sixth century and is still in use today.

near the church in what is considered holy ground. So you see, the church is a part of our life from cradle to grave.

I'm talking about the Roman Catholic Church, of course, the only church in Western Europe. Everyone I know believes in God and follows the teachings of His son, Jesus Christ. But sometimes in our city you'll meet people of two other prominent faiths of our time. They are Jews and Muslims. We have fought many wars with the Muslims, the followers of Islam. The Holy Lands in and around Jerusalem have long been important to both faiths, and for 200 years the Pope and the Church have blessed a series of battles to take back these lands from the Muslims. These wars were called the Crusades, and the last one ended only 30 years ago, in 1272.

We have many churches in our city. Some are plain and simple and others are more detailed. But the biggest and most beautiful of all is the cathedral. Come, follow me and I'll show you!

See it there? The roof reaches up to 80 feet high! It's so big it makes all the other buildings in the city look small. It's even taller than the city walls, so you can see it from miles away.[1]

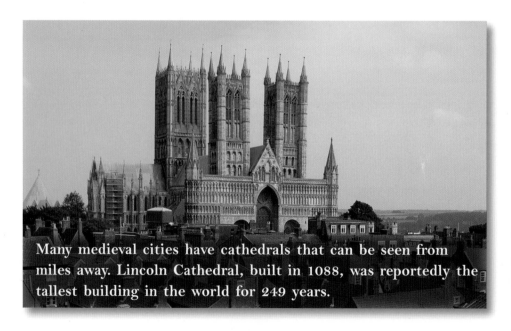

Many medieval cities have cathedrals that can be seen from miles away. Lincoln Cathedral, built in 1088, was reportedly the tallest building in the world for 249 years.

Masons and artisans worked long and hard to build this cathedral because they believe this work is holy. Let's open the heavy wooden doors so you can see inside. The cathedral is filled with carvings, paintings, and stained-glass windows. The stained-glass windows are beautiful, but they also have an important purpose. Many people can't read and when we go to Mass, the service is held in Latin, a language most people don't understand. But the windows in the church show stories from the Bible. We can look at the windows and see pictures of events important to our faith, like the birth, death, and resurrection of Christ.

Do you see that man walking across the sanctuary with the long robe and the odd haircut? He's a monk and he lives in the monastery. He has taken a vow of poverty, which means he can't own anything, and a vow of chastity, which means he will never get married and have children. His haircut, short on the sides and with the top of his head shaved, is called a tonsure. Monks do a variety of jobs. They teach, give to the poor, care for the ill, and look after travelers. They also spend many long hours copying books like the Bible by hand.

Women who devote themselves to the church are called nuns and live in convents. They wear long robes called habits. Often these women entered the convent as young girls so they could be taught by the nuns, who are well educated. They spend their lives praying, studying, and helping the ill.

Others who work in the church are bishops, priests, and friars. Bishops are appointed by the Pope to look after the needs of people in a large area called a diocese. The priest works in the local church, leading worship services and performing ceremonies like baptisms and weddings. Friars travel between villages, towns and cities, preaching the Word of God and doing good deeds. They have given up all their things and live by begging.

The most important and powerful person in the Church is the Pope. We believe that the Pope is second only to God because he is God's assistant on Earth. He is not only the leader of our faith but he also has

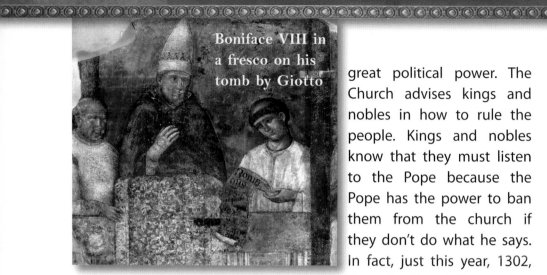

Boniface VIII in a fresco on his tomb by Giotto

great political power. The Church advises kings and nobles in how to rule the people. Kings and nobles know that they must listen to the Pope because the Pope has the power to ban them from the church if they don't do what he says. In fact, just this year, 1302, Pope Boniface VIII gave the order called Unam Sanctam. It says the Pope has complete rule over the Church and all kings and rulers. Everyone must obey the Pope's wishes to be given salvation. Those who do will go to Heaven.

Kings and nobles give land and money to the Church, making it very wealthy. The Church also takes a tithe of the peasants' and merchants' profits. That means people like my father give one-tenth of their wealth to the Church. The Church also gains wealth from the sale of indulgences. An indulgence is a paper given by a church official that says a person has been excused from a sin.

This money helps the Church set up charities, schools, and hospitals. But much of the money goes to benefit the powerful people in the church, like the Pope, cardinals, and bishops. They often live in luxury, unlike the monks, nuns, and friars who live in poverty.

Many churches and cathedrals, like this one, were built to honor saints. We believe that saints are holy people who have died but who now live in Heaven with God. They can ask God to perform miracles, such as curing the ill or making crops grow. We pray to saints and ask them to help and protect us. Many people go on long journeys, called pilgrimages, to visit places where saints are buried or where objects belonging to them are kept. These objects are called relics. Sometimes they're pieces of a saint's body, like a finger or tooth!

Let's slip quietly out of the cathedral now and continue on our way around the city. Are you ready to see the castle? Let's go!

How did Protestantism Begin?

The Roman Catholic Church was the only denomination of Christianity throughout the Middle Ages. This changed when, on October 31, 1517, a priest named Martin Luther posted his now-famous 95 Theses on the door of Castle Church in Wittenberg, Germany.

In his Theses, Luther spoke against the dishonesty of the Church. His biggest concern was the Church's sale of indulgences for the forgiveness of sins. The Church had gained much of its money by doing this.[2]

But Luther thought being excused from sins by buying indulgences denied the biblical teaching of forgiveness and salvation by faith alone. Because Luther disagreed with many other parts of Catholic teachings, including the power of the Pope, he thought the Church needed to be changed and that it could be done only by making a new body of Christians. The movement Luther started became known as the Reformation.

The 95 Theses were written in German and widely copied and printed. Within two weeks they had spread throughout Germany, and within two months throughout Europe. This was one of the first events in history that was strongly affected by the printing press, which made the spread of documents easier.

In 1521, Pope Leo X formally excommunicated Luther from the Church. But Luther had many followers who also wanted to see change in the Church. Because they "protested" what they saw as dishonesty in the Church, they became known as Protestants.

The Protestant Reformation began in England in 1534 when King Henry VIII named himself head of the Christian Church there. Since that time England has formally been a Protestant nation.

CHAPTER 4
Castles, Nobles, and Knights

There's the castle! That's quite a house for one noble family, isn't it? But the castle isn't just a home; it's a fortress! Inside those large stone walls is a whole busy community, with everyone working for the good of the kingdom.

Before we go inside, take a look at the notched walls and guard towers. See how the walls have edges that go up and down? The raised sections are called merlons and the gaps are called crenels. When the castle is under attack, archers position themselves along the wall walks and fire their arrows through the crenels. The merlons shelter them from enemy fire. The guard towers are always manned by sentries who are looking out for enemies.

Since castles house the most important people in the kingdom—whether that be the king, a baron, a duke, a count, or other nobleman—they are the places most subject to attack. For that reason, it isn't easy to get into them. Most castles have only one way in, and that begins with the gatehouse.

One of the many castles built by King William I is Warwick Castle in the country town of Warwickshire. It was built in 1068, just two years after William—formerly the Duke of Normandy—conquered England at the Battle of Hastings.

This portcullis, or latticed grill, secures the entrance to Carlisle Castle. An important part of any castle's defense, the portcullis is raised and lowered by the gatehouse guards using chains or ropes.

Our gatehouse is three stories tall and heavily guarded. Part of the guards' job is working the portcullis. This is the grilled gate that acts as a door, except that it moves up and down. The guards have to lift the portcullis so we can move through the gate and walk on the drawbridge over the moat that surrounds the castle. In case of attack, the drawbridge will be lifted, and entrance to the castle is cut off.

Now that we're inside the first wall, the first thing you'll notice is the smell! Yes, it's the stables. Hundreds of horses are housed here. Most days the men, called grooms, who take care of the horses, will take them to the exercise yard, which is a bare patch of earth beside the moat. The horses have a number of important jobs. The fast, lean horses are used by messengers. The big strong horses are used by knights to ride into battle.

We're in luck! Some of the knights are out riding their horses, preparing for the tournament. I'll take you to it soon. Everyone from king to peasant will be there because the tournaments are such great fun! But first let me tell you something about the knights themselves.

I'll start at the beginning. You'll notice the boys who are over there helping the knights. They're called pages. Because they were born into noble families, they have the chance to become knights themselves. At the age of seven or eight, a page is sent to work with a knight for about seven years. Not only does he help take care of his lord but he learns how to ride, fight, hunt with hawks, and everything else that's involved in serving the kingdom as a knight.

At 14 or 15 years old, a page becomes a squire. Squires begin serious training for combat. In fact, a squire will lead his lord's horse into combat and will hold the horse for him when he fights on foot. At home, the squire still waits on his lord and is entrusted with many important tasks.

Finally, after finishing the long years of training and proving himself worthy of the title, the squire becomes a knight. Knights are the most important warriors on the battlefield. Many other soldiers fight for the king, most of them foot soldiers gathered from the local countryside. But one knight—with his protective armor, his powerful horse, and his many deadly weapons—is worth ten ordinary soldiers.[1] The knight is required to fight for 40 days a year for his own lord, but he often fights more than that.

Knights gallop into battle wearing 55 to 80 pounds of armor and carrying a lance, a long spear-like weapon that is

A page waits on his knight.

A knight gallops into battle thoroughly equipped with years of training, a full suit of protective armor, and a wide variety of deadly weapons.

nine to 14 feet long.[2] On his belt he may also carry a two-handed sword on one side and a dagger on the other. He may also have a battle-ax, another sword, or a club-headed mace (a spiked metal ball) attached to his saddle. Even his horse wears armor in battle.

All of the weapons and armor are made here in the castle, in a place called the armory. The armorer and his apprentice make swords, lances, and shields for the knights as well as daggers, axes, and maces for the foot soldiers.

The knights have their own living spaces in the towers of the castles. While sparsely decorated, the spaces are much nicer than the barracks where the hundreds of foot soldiers live. The knights have beds while the soldiers sleep only on mats or rough straw mattresses. Since the soldiers rarely wash, the barracks don't smell much better than the stables!

Knights live by a code of honor called chivalry. The Church established the rules of chivalry to make sure knights behave properly, set a good example, and don't mistreat the people. A knight should be brave, loyal, generous, polite, and honest. He must protect widows and children and defend and be faithful to the Church.

Now let's pass through the inner wall of the castle and take a look at some of the more important places. If we climb the spiral staircase way up to the top of one of the largest towers, we'll come to the master's bedroom. The master is lord of the castle. He sleeps in that big four-poster bed with the heavy linen curtains. The curtains keep out drafts and give the lord some privacy. Many servants wait on him and even sleep in his bedroom, but the most important servant of the lord's bedchamber is a noble called the chamberlain. He is the first to greet the lord in the morning and the last to bid him goodnight.

In our castle, ordinary meals are taken in a dining hall called a refectory. But when the lord entertains guests and it's time for a

The lord sleeps in a four-poster bed with heavy linen curtains that help keep out drafts. This master bedroom is in the Tower of London.

banquet, such feasts are enjoyed in a grand room called the Great Hall. See how long it is, and how tall the ceiling is! The lord, his lady, and their most important guests sit on a raised platform. Trumpets announce the arrival of food. Sometimes more than 60 dishes are served at banquets. In addition to pastries, bread, fruit, and cheese, the menu will include many kinds of meats, fish, and shellfish.

The high balcony at the end of the Great Hall is called a gallery. That's where musicians play and minstrels sing. The harp and lute are popular instruments. For entertainment, the lord may also call on his jester. The jester is good at making his master laugh. He arrives in his tri-pointed hat with bells and his shoes with long, turned-up toes. He tells stories and jokes, juggles, and acts as a mime.

All the delicious food for the banquet is prepared in the castle's kitchen. This lower level room is a hive of activity! The cook plans meals, shouts orders, and tastes the food before it leaves the kitchen. The undercooks prepare vegetables, pluck birds, knead dough, and answer to the cook. Beneath the undercooks are the kitchen boys, or scullions, who do little jobs like stirring the stew or washing the dishes. The cook

Steep stone steps lead down to the cells in the dungeon of Warwick Castle.

and undercooks use cast-iron or copper pots and make the food over an open fire. Like most castles, ours has a kitchen garden which includes fruit trees, vines, and vegetables. Herbs and other plants are used at the hospital. Yes, we have a hospital here in the castle. Let's go look at it.

It's a quiet room, isn't it? It is long and narrow and lined with cots. The hospital is run by the Church. That's why you see monks and nuns taking care of patients, though, of course, there are doctors here too. Many different herbs are used to treat pain and to heal wounds. Sometimes patients are bled; that is, a small cut is made on the patient's arm to let the "bad blood" drain out. Doctors often look at a patient's urine. They use a urine chart to make a diagnosis from the color.

The monks and nuns believe in miracles, so they spend time praying for the ill. Right outside the hospital is the chapel. When you step into the chapel, you'll notice that the light is dim and the chapel smells of incense. At the far end of the room is the altar with its gold cross. With its stained-glass windows and the colorful frescoes (paintings) on the walls, the chapel is the most beautiful room in the castle. It has its own priest, who stays busy leading Mass and prayers. He also hears confessions, performs last rites for the dying, and blesses the knights who are about to go into battle.

While the chapel sits high up so as to be close to God, there's an underground place in the castle where the dwellers might think God has forgotten them. Let's climb down these steep stone steps to the dungeon. This is where the prisoners are housed in cells. The cells are dark and filled with rats and cockroaches. The prisoners are given very little food and are sometimes allowed to starve. A prisoner might spend months or even years in this place. You don't want to be an enemy of the lord!

Enough of the dungeon. We need to leave the castle now. The tournament is about to begin and we don't want to be late!

FIVE FAMOUS KINGS OF ENGLAND

William the Conqueror—King of England: 1066–1087. William the Conqueror was not an Englishman but a Norman. He was Duke of Normandy when he conquered England at the Battle of Hastings in 1066. He was crowned King William I of England in January 1067 at Westminster Abbey, London.[3]

William loved to build castles. In the early Middle Ages castles sprang up all over Europe, but there were very few in England. After William became king, this began to change. By 1100, there were more than 500 castles in England where once there had only been six. One of William's best-known fortresses is the Tower of London.[4]

King Richard I, also known as Richard the Lionheart—King of England: 1189–1199. King Richard earned his nickname because of his great bravery. He was a fearless warrior and spent much of his reign on the battlefields of Europe. Perhaps he is best known for his leadership during the Third Crusade when the Christians once again battled the Muslims for the Holy Land.[5]

The time of King Richard the Lionheart is the setting for the popular children's story *Robin Hood*.

King John—King of England: 1199–1216. King John took the throne of England after his brother, Richard the Lionheart. He was a cruel leader who made his subjects unhappy. One day, a group of nobles met and wrote the Magna Carta, or Great Charter. This charter limited the power of the king and gave more freedom to the people. King John was forced to sign it in 1215, a year before his death.[6]

King Edward I—King of England: 1272–1307. While still a prince, Edward was a leader of the Ninth Crusade. He returned home from the Holy Land when his father, King Henry III, died. After Edward was crowned king, he accepted the *Magna Carta* and under his reign England grew prosperous. He is perhaps best known for conquering Wales and building Welsh castles.[7]

King Henry V—King of England: 1413–1422. King Henry V was a beloved leader among the English. He was devoted to the Church, gave freely to the poor, and was known as a kind man in both word and deed. He was a brave warrior and cared greatly about the men he led into battle in France during the Hundred Years War. He is perhaps best known for winning the Battle of Agincourt.[8]

CHAPTER 5
Tournaments, Plays and Holy Days

We're going outside the city walls for the tournament, to the big fields past the farms where there's enough room to hold the games. Because the week-long tournaments are the greatest of all sporting events, everybody comes. You can see the crowds now! And all the tents! Vendors are here selling food. Merchants are selling their goods. Storytellers, minstrels, and acrobats are wandering around, looking for an audience and hoping to tuck some coins in their purses. You can see all sorts of games going on, like stone-throwing contests, wrestling matches, and dice games. As we walk around, beware of the pickpockets! We call them "cutpurses" here, and they're very good at making their living by stealing.

Now that we're all gathered together, you can see the different kinds of clothes. There are laws about what kind of clothes each class of people may wear, so that wealthy merchants

The tournament is a week-long festival of games, feasting, singing, dancing, and jousting.

aren't confused with nobles and craftspeople aren't confused with wealthy merchants. Up there in the stands are the lords and ladies, showing off their jeweled clothes of crimson and green and cloth of gold. Only these most powerful nobles are allowed to wear gold or silver cloth. And only they may wear purple silk, as only they can afford it. All of their clothes are made for them by tailors.

For those of us who are working folks and peasants, though, our clothes are homemade and dyed in drab colors. The cloth is wool or coarse linen. Unlike the fashions worn by the lords and ladies, our clothes are simple. Men wear tunics that come down to mid-thigh over pairs of stockings. Women wear rough sleeveless tunics over dresses with sleeves. Sometimes a hood is wound around their heads for warmth, or women may wear kerchiefs. The clothes of the peasants must last for many years, and are often patched and mended.

I'll tell you a secret about the young ladies up in the stands. Each has come to cheer on her favorite knight, and she's dressed in her finest, hoping to impress him with her beauty. At the same time, the knight is ready to show off for his lady and to prove himself not only worthy of battle but of the young lady's love. Sometimes a lady will give a knight her scarf or glove to show that he's her "special knight." Tournaments celebrate not only military skill but also romantic love. In fact, if you read some of the poems and stories that are being written today, you'll find they often talk about the love of a noble for his lady. These odes are written not in Latin but in our own language, and they're becoming very popular.

But let's get back to the games. There are two main events. One is jousting, in which one knight fights another. And the other is the mock battle, or melee, in which groups of knights fight each other just like on the battlefield. The tournaments can be nearly as dangerous as war, with many knights wounded and even killed. But that doesn't stop the knights; they love fighting!

The trumpets tell us it's time for the first round of jousting. Here come the knights, wearing special armor sparkling with gold and brightly painted with their colors and emblems. Even their helmets are decked out with plumes. Their horses wear armor and linens of bright colors.

The first two knights are chosen. They face each other from a great distance, ready to charge. When the signal is given, the horses gallop. Hoof beats thunder over the ground. The two riders speed toward each other with lances raised. When they reach each other, we hear the loud clash of lances against armor and one of the knights falls from his horse. We have our first victor! The tournament will last for days because all these knights will have a chance to joust until we have a champion.

The tournaments aren't our only form of fun and entertainment. Throughout the year our long working days are broken up with plenty of holy days, pageants, feasts, and fairs. Dozens of saints' days are celebrated as religious festivals, and on those days we enjoy special church services, plays, and parades. Often we gather in the marketplace, and along with the usual buying and selling there are all sorts of activities like wrestling, dancing, ball games, cockfighting, and bearbaiting (dogs attacking a chained bear).

Christmas is the merriest season of the year, with events lasting up to two weeks as we celebrate the birth of Christ. Several saints' days are celebrated the week before Christmas. The Feast of the Holy Innocents falls on December 28. Christ's baptism and the visit of the Magi are honored on Epiphany, January 6, which is the Twelfth Night of Christmas. We decorate our homes with holly and ivy, burn the Yule log, exchange gifts and eat plenty of special foods like spice cake and roast goose. We fill the wassail bowl with ale, roasted apples, spiced cloves, ginger, nutmeg, and cinnamon, and drink a toast to family and friends.[1]

Whitsuntide is another favorite holiday because it marks the end of the long winter and the beginning of spring. It falls on the seventh Sunday after Easter, which is almost always in May. People take long walks in the woods and meadows to gather flowers, apple blossoms, and green leaves to decorate homes. Festivities for Whitsuntide include circling the maypole and singing songs like "Sumer is icumen in."[2]

Many English towns and cities like ours have plays that are performed in squares and marketplaces around the feast of Corpus Christi, which is 54 days after Easter. There are two kinds: the mystery plays are about the life of Christ and the miracle plays are based on stories of the Bible. These plays were started by priests in the tenth century because they are a good way for people to learn about the Bible. Now the plays are more detailed, with all sorts of fancy costumes and scenery. They often begin with the actors making a grand parade through the city streets.

Each play is put on by a certain guild, and the guild members play the parts. The guild may choose a play that's related to their craft. For example, the fishmongers perform *Jonah and the Whale* and the shipwrights put on *Noah's Ark.* Men play all the roles, since acting is considered improper for women.

With all the holidays, plays, feasts, and pageants, you can see that while our lives are filled with long days of hard work, they are also filled with many hours of great fun. Now, let's get back to the jousting!

MEDIEVAL LITERATURE

Stories have been handed down for generations since the beginning of time. Up until the fourteenth century, though, stories were largely passed along by word of mouth. Even through most of the Middle Ages, people relied on storytellers and minstrels to entertain them with spoken word and song. This slowly changed in the fourteenth century when people began to keep records and write down history, poems, and stories in their own languages, such as English and French, rather than in Latin.

As more and more people learned how to read, they found literature to be an enjoyable pastime. But even those who couldn't read were able to enjoy communal readings, in which a group gathered to listen as someone read a book aloud.[3]

Many fourteenth-century kings and queens were book-lovers, leading the way in making reading popular. Queen Isabella, wife of King Edward II, collected many volumes of books, including prayer missals, encyclopedias, history books, and romances. She also borrowed books from the royal lending library. The library was kept in the Tower of London and held at least 340 volumes. Of course, these books were actually handwritten. Printed books didn't exist in England until the 1460s.

Much of what we know about the Middle Ages comes from the poems and stories written during that time, such as William Langland's *Piers Plowman* and Boccaccio's *Decameron*. Perhaps the best-known work to come from fourteenth-century England is Geoffrey Chaucer's *Canterbury Tales*, a long poem that offers great insights into the people and everyday life of Medieval England. Considered by many to be the height of medieval literature, *Canterbury Tales* is still being read and enjoyed today.

Imagine that: stories, poems, and plays that were written hundreds of years ago are still adored by readers like you.

CE

476	Romulus Augustulus, the last Western Roman emperor, is overthrown. The Middle Ages begin with the collapse of the Roman Empire.
500–900	New kingdoms are set up throughout England and Europe as tribes from Northern Europe move into the old Roman lands and take over.
900–1000	First castles are built in Europe, in northern France.
1066	Duke William of Normandy defeats Harold II of England at the Battle of Hastings. William is crowned King of England. He brings feudalism and culture from France to England.
1095	Pope Urban II calls on the Christian knights and nobles of Europe to recapture the Holy Land from the Muslims. The First Crusade begins the following year. There will be nine Crusades in all, with the era of the Crusades ending in 1291.
1215	King John of England signs the Magna Carta, giving basic rights to people and limiting the power of the king.
1315–1317	The Great Famine devastates western Europe. Ten to fifteen percent of the population of Europe dies of starvation and disease.
1337	The Hundred Years War between England and France begins.
1348–1351	The plague known as the Black Death sweeps through Europe. Thousands die, including an estimated one out of every five persons in England. A second wave of the plague strikes from 1361 to 1362.
1400–1550	The Middle Ages begin to wane as the Renaissance Era begins in Italy and spreads throughout Europe.
1455	First book is printed in Europe on Johannes Gutenberg's printing press.
1492	Christopher Columbus sets sail from Spain, discovering what will later be known as the Americas.

Chapter 2. Work and Livelihood

1. Walter Buehr, *When Towns Had Walls: Life in a Medieval English Town* (New York: Thomas Y. Crowell Company, 1970), p. 91.

2. Ibid., p. 92.

3. Ian Mortimer, *The Time Traveler's Guide to Medieval England* (New York: Touchstone, a Division of Simon & Schuster, Inc., 2008), p. 9.

4. Frances and Joseph Gies, *Cathedral, Forge, and Waterwheel: Technology and Invention in the Middle Ages* (New York: HarperCollins Publishers, 1994), pp. 44–45.

5. Mortimer, pp. 83–84.

6. Gies, p. 175.

7 Ibid., p. 227.

8. Ibid., pp. 201–202.

9. Ibid., pp. 242, 246.

Chapter 3. The Church and Society

1. Ian Mortimer, *The Time Traveler's Guide to Medieval England* (New York: Touchstone, a Division of Simon & Schuster, Inc., 2008), p. 7.

2. "Martin Luther Posts 95 Theses," History.com, accessed on 6/11/2012, http://www.history.com/this-day-in-history/martin-luther-posts-95-theses

Chapter 4. Castles, Nobles, and Knights

1. "Medieval Swords and Armor," *Medieval Life and Times,* accessed on 6/12/2012, http://www.medieval-life-and-times.info/medieval-swords-and-armor/index.htm

2. "Lance," *The Middle Ages,* accessed on 6/12/2012, http://www.middle-ages.org.uk/lance.htm

3. "William the Conqueror," *Medieval Life and Times,* accessed on 6/13/2012, http://www.medieval-life-and-times.info/medieval-kings/william-the-conqueror-biography.htm

4. Ibid.

5. "Richard the Lionheart," *Medieval Life and Times,* accessed on 6/13/2012, http://www.medieval-life-and-times-info/medieval-kings/richard-the-lionheart-biography.htm

6. "King John," *Medieval Life and Times,* accessed on 6/13/2012, http://www.medieval-life-and-times.info/medieval-kings/king-john-biography.htm

7. "King Edward I," *Medieval Life and Times,* accessed on 6/13/2012, http://www.medieval-life-and-times.info/medieval-kings/king-edward-i-biography.htm

8. "King Henry V," *Medieval Life and Times,* accessed on 6/13/2012, http://www.medieval-life-and-times.info/medieval-kings/king-henry-v-biography.htm

Chapter 5. Tournaments, Plays, and Holy Days

1. Walter Buehr, *When Towns Had Walls: Life in a Medieval English Town* (New York: Thomas Y. Crowell Company, 1970), pp. 155–156.

2. Ibid., 158.

3. Ian Mortimer, *The Time Traveler's Guide to Medieval England* (New York: Touchstone, a Division of Simon & Schuster, Inc., 2008), p. 274.

Books

Eastwood, Kay. *Medieval Society.* New York: Crabtree Publishing Company, 2004.

Galloway, Priscilla. *Archers, Alchemists, and 98 Other Medieval Jobs You Might Have Loved or Loathed.* New York: Annick Press Ltd., 2003.

Hibbert, Clare. *Look Around a Medieval Castle.* Mankato, Minnesota: Arcturus Publishing Ltd., 2008.

Hinds, Kathryn. *Life in the Middle Ages: The Castle.* New York: Benchmark Books, Marshall Cavendish Corporation, 2001.

———. *Life in the Middle Ages: The City.* New York: Benchmark Books, Marshall Cavendish Corporation, 2001.

Johnson, Sheri. *Kids in the Medieval World.* Mankato, Minnesota: Capstone Press, Capstone Publishers, 2009.

Schlitz, Laura Amy. *Good Masters! Sweet Ladies! Voices from a Medieval Village.* Cambridge, Massachusetts: Candlewick Press, 2007.

Works Consulted

Buehr, Walter. *When Towns Had Walls: Life in a Medieval English Town.* New York: Thomas Y. Crowell Company, 1970.

Gies, Frances, and Joseph Gies. *Cathedral, Forge, and Waterwheel: Technology and Invention in the Middle Ages.* New York: HarperCollins Publishers, 1994.

———. *Daily Life in Medieval Times.* New York: Black Dog & Leventhal Publishers, Inc., 1969, 1974, 1990.

"Martin Luther Posts 95 Theses," History.com, accessed on 6/11/2012, http://www.history.com/this-day-in-history/martin-luther-posts-95-theses

Medieval Life and Times
     http://www.medieval-life-and-times.info/

The Middle Ages
     http://www.middle-ages.org.uk/

Mortimer, Ian. *The Time Traveler's Guide to Medieval England.* New York: Touchstone, a Division of Simon & Schuster, Inc., 2008.

Orme, Nicholas. *Medieval Children.* New Haven, Connecticut: Yale University Press, 2001.

On the Internet

Britain Express: Medieval England
     http://www.britainexpress.com/History/medieval_britain_index.htm

Medieval Spell: The Medieval History Source
     http://www.medieval-spell.com/

A Study of the Middle Ages: Presented by Sir Richard Dragon Tamer
     http://sirdragontamer.com/MA_index.html

apprentice (uh-PREN-tis)—A child who learned a craft or trade by working with an adult who was a master craftsmen. This training usually lasted seven years.

chivalry (SHIV-ul-ree)—The unwritten code of conduct followed by a knight. This included being brave, loyal, generous, and honest.

clergy (KLUR-jee)—The body of people ordained for religious duties in the Christian Church.

Crusades (KREW-sayds)—A number of expeditions by Christian knights who wanted to take back the Holy Land from the Muslims.

denomination (deh-NOM-ih-nay-shun)—A group or branch of any religion.

diagnosis (DY-ig-noh-sys)—The labeling of an illness or other problem by looking at symptoms.

distaff (DYS-tiff)—A stick or spindle onto which wool is wound for spinning.

excommunicate (eks-kuh-MYOO-nuh-kayt)—To cut off from membership in the Church.

famine (FAH-min)—Extreme shortage of food.

feudalism (FYOO-dul-ih-zum)—The Medieval system of organizing society where wealthy and powerful landowners gave land to people of lower classes in return for their loyalty.

fief (FEEF)—A part of land, especially one held on the condition of feudal service.

furrow—A long, narrow trench made in the ground by a plow, especially for planting seeds.

guild (GILD)—A group of people in the same craft or trade. A guild took care of the welfare of its members and set standards for training and workmanship.

journeyman (JUR-nee-man)—A worker who finished his apprenticeship and traveled from town to town working in his trade, preparing to become a master craftsman.

knight (NITE)—A man trained to fight as a heavily-armed warrior on horseback. Knights were important rulers as well.

merchant (MUR-chint)—Someone who made a living by buying and selling things.

missal—A prayer book.

noble (NOH-bull)—An important person who controlled a lot of land and ruled large numbers of people.

page—A boy in the first stage of training to become a knight.

peasant (PEH-zint)—A poor person who owns or rents a small piece of land for farming.

plague (PLAYG)—A widespread and often deadly disease that is easily spread from person to person.

Pope—The leader of the Roman Catholic Church.

saint (SAYNT)—A person seen by the Catholic Church as someone who is holy and able to perform miracles both in life and after death.

serf—A peasant who could not refuse to give both labor and money to a lord.

squire (SKWYRE)—A teen boy who served a knight by carrying his armor and weapons, preparing to become a knight himself.

tithe (TYTHE)—Tax taken for the support of the Church and its clergy.

vassal—A person who received protection and land from a lord in return for loyalty and service.